The Blueprint to Raspberry Pi 3

A Beginners Guide: Everything You Need to Know for Starting Your Own Projects

By: CyberPunk Architects

This book is copyright protected. This is only for personal use. You cannot amend, distribute, sell, use, quote or paraphrase any part or the content within this book without the consent of the author or copyright owner. Legal action will be pursued if this is breached.

Disclaimer Notice:

Please note the information contained within this document is for educational and entertainment purposes only. Every attempt has been made to provide accurate, up to date and reliable complete information. No warranties of any kind are expressed or implied. Readers acknowledge that the author is not engaging in the rendering of legal, financial, medical or professional advice.

By reading this document, the reader agrees that under no circumstances are we responsible for any losses, direct or indirect, which are incurred as a result of the use of information contained within this document, including, but not limited to, — errors, omissions, or inaccuracies.

Table Of Contents

Introduction

Thank you for downloading my book *"Raspberry Pi: The Blueprint for Raspberry Pi 3: Everything You Need to Know for Starting Your Own Projects"*. Recently the Raspberry Pi has been receiving a ton of press coverage and capturing the curiosity of people all around the world, at least people who are technology journalists and enthusiasts. As time has passed, more and more people have heard of this fascinating small single board computer stamped with chips and connectors, but many people aren't sure exactly what it is.

If you are one of those people who is intrigued by the tastily named Raspberry Pi, this book is for you. In this book, we are going to look at a quick overview of what the Raspberry Pi is, and then we are going to break down the specifications and what they mean. Finally, we are going to look at all the amazing projects the Raspberry Pi can assist you with. Whether you are well-versed in technology or diving into it for the first time, this book is going to help you.

By the time, you are done reading this book, you are going to have the knowledge to use your Raspberry Pi with ease to do anything from watching a movie to playing games, and from creating a spreadsheet to learning how to program.

Chapter 1: Raspberry Pi – An Overview

The Raspberry Pi has many incredible features. The largest appeal of the Raspberry Pi computer is that it is a small size, and is also affordable. The Raspberry Pi can be used as a traditional computer by simply being plugged into a TV and a keyboard. Since 2012, there have been many models of the Raspberry Pi released to the public, each with their own improvements and changes.

Approximately the size of a credit card and available for as little as $5USD, the intended purpose of the Raspberry Pi was to bring affordable computer options to everyone. Below, we are going to take a brief look at the different models of Raspberry Pi.

Raspberry Pi 1 Model A – This was the original model of the Raspberry Pi. Released in February 2012. This was followed up late by the Raspberry Pi 1 Model A Plus which was released in November 2014, which featured a larger hard drive and a lower price point.

Raspberry Pi 1 Model B– The Generation 1 and 1 Plus of the Model B Raspberry Pi were released in April 2012 and July 2014 respectively. The 1 Plus had a lower price point than the original Model B and featured a microSD slot instead of the standard SD slot.

Raspberry Pi Zero – This was a smaller model that was released in November 2015. The size of the Zero was smaller and it had a reduced input and output. This is the cheapest model of Raspberry Pi that is currently available for purchase. The original Zero did not include video input. However, a second version released in May 2016 included video input options similar to other models.

Raspberry Pi 2 – This model included more ram than any of the previous models and was released in February 2015. This model is at the high end of all Raspberry Pi products and can be found for just $35USD.

Raspberry Pi 3 Model B – This is the newest model of Raspberry Pi. Released in February 2016, the Raspberry Pi 3, Model B is bundled with the additions including onboard Wi-Fi, Bluetooth, and

USB boot capabilities. We will cover more on this later in this book.

There are a few things that are common among all the versions of Raspberry Pi. This includes the Broadcom system on a chip, which features a CPU (Central Processing System) that is compatible with ARM, as well as on-chip GPU (Graphics Processing Unit).

The boards all have between one and four USB slots, as well as an HDMI slot, composite video output and a 3.5 mm phone jack for audio capabilities.

The creators of Raspberry Pi provide *Raspbian*, which is a Debian-based Linux distribution for download. It also provides third party *Ubuntu*, *Windows 10* IOT Core, RISC OS, and other specialized media center distributions. While the Raspberry Pi supports many programming languages, it promotes Python and Scratch as its main programming language. You also have the option of open source or closed source firmware, although the default firmware is closed source.

Chapter 2: Raspberry Pi 3 – Model B Hardware Specifications

There have been several evolutions in the hardware that the Raspberry Pi offers. In this chapter, we are going to focus on the Raspberry Pi 3 – Model B specifically.

For the purpose of keeping this book easy to read for those of you who aren't as familiar with the technological jargon, while keeping it interesting for those of you who don't need as in depth of an explanation, this chapter is going to be broken down into sections that allow you to skim through and find the information you are looking for without having to read every explanation.

Wireless Radio – Broadcom BCM43438

This wireless radio has been expertly built directly into the board to keep the cost of the Raspberry Pi down. It is also so small; you are going to be able to see the markings through a microscope or magnifying glass. The Broadcom BCM43438 chip gives the Raspberry Pi 2.4 GHZ 802.11n wireless LAN, Bluetooth Low Energy, and Bluetooth 4.1 Classic radio support. This is what is going to allow you to connect your Raspberry Pi to the internet, both through a wired connection as well as through a wireless connection.

SoC – Broadcom BCM2837

This SoC (System on Chip) has been built specifically for the Raspberry Pi 3 – Model B. This SoC features four high-performance ARM Cortex-A53 processing cores which run at 1.2GHz and have 32kB level one and 512kB level two memory. It also has a Video Core IV graphics processor and is also linked to the one gigabyte LPDDR2 memory module that is located on the rear of the board.

GPIO – 40-Pin Header, Populated

The GPIO (General Purpose Input Output) header is the same on this Raspberry Pi as it has been going back through most of the Raspberry Pi models. This means that any existing GPIO hardware is going to work with the Raspberry Pi 3 – Model B without any further modifications needed. The only change that has been made to this part of the Raspberry Pi is a change to which UART is exposed on the pins. However, this doesn't affect usage as the operating system internally handles it.

USB Chip – SMSC LAN9514

This is another part of the Raspberry Pi that hasn't changed from the Raspberry Pi 2. The SMSC LAN9514 adds 10/100 Ethernet connectivity as well as four USB channels to the board. The chip connects to the SoC through a single USB channel, acting as a USB to Ethernet adaptor as well as a USB hub.

To sum up all the information above:

SoC: Broadcom BCM2837

CPU: 4× ARM Cortex-A53, 1.2GHz

GPU: Broadcom VideoCore IV

RAM: 1GB LPDDR2 (900 MHz)

Networking: 10/100 Ethernet, 2.4GHz 802.11n wireless

Bluetooth: Bluetooth 4.1 Classic, Bluetooth Low Energy

Storage: microSD

GPIO: 40-pin header, populated

Ports: HDMI, 3.5mm analog audio-video jack, 4×
USB 2.0, Ethernet, Camera Serial Interface (CSI),
Display Serial Interface (DSI)

Now that we are all familiar with the hardware that
is inside the Raspberry Pi 3 – Model B, we are going
to have a look at the software.

Chapter 3: Raspberry Pi 3 – Software Specifications

One of the neat things about the Raspberry Pi 3 – Model B is that you can run almost any software on it. While it primarily uses *Raspbian*, which is a Debian-based Linux operating system, you are not limited to using this. In this chapter, we are going to run through all the different operating systems, driver APIs, firmware and other third party application software that will be accessible to you for use on the Raspberry Pi 3 – Model B.

Operating Systems

On the official Raspberry Pi website, you will have access to Ubuntu Mate, Snappy Ubuntu Core, Windows 10 IoT Core, and RISC OS, as well as specialized distributions for the Kodi media center and classroom management. Below we are going to cover every operating system that can be used, categorized by those that are Linux based and those that not Linux based.

Linux Based Operating Systems:

Alpine Linux – This is a Linux distribution that is based on *musl* and *BusyBox*. It has been primarily designed for those power users who require more security, simplicity, and resource efficiency.

Android Things – This is an embedded version of the Android operating system that is designed for IoT device development.

Ark OS – This operating system has been designed for website and email self-hosting.

CentOS – This is a newer operating system that is only available for Raspberry Pi 2 and newer.

Diet Pi – This operating system includes a diverse range of servers that are ideal for media, Minecraft, VPN, and much more.

Fedora 25 – This is another newer operating system that is only available for the newer Raspberry Pi models.

Gentoo – This operating system is ideal for users who want full control of the software that they use on their Raspberry Pi 3.

Instant WebKiosk – This operating system is ideal for users who are looking for digital signage purposes such as web and media views.

<u>Kali Linux</u> – This operating system is a Debian derived distro that has been designed for digital forensics and penetration testing.

<u>Kano OS</u> – This operating system is one that you can build and customize to be exactly what you want it to be for you. Completely free, this is a great choice if you want to have full control over your operating system.

<u>MinePeon</u> – This operating system has been designed to be dedicated to mining cryptocurrency.

<u>Moebius</u> – This is another operating system that is based on Debian. This operating system is a light ARM HF distribution that uses Raspbian repository but fits onto a 128 MB SD card. This operating system only offers minimal services and has had its memory use optimized to keep it small.

<u>NARD SDK</u> – This is a software development kids that is intended for industrial embedded systems.

<u>OpenSUSE</u> – This is another operating system that gives you full control over creating the code for your system.

<u>OpenWrt</u> – This operating system is primarily used to route network traffic on embedded devices.

<u>Pardus ARM</u> – This operating system is another option for a Debian derived system. This is the light

version of the Pardus operating system that is popular with the Turkish Government.

Pidora – This is a Fedora Remix that has been optimized for use on the Raspberry Pi.

ROKOS – This operating system is another Rasbian based option that is integrated for use with Bitcoin and OKCash cryptocurrencies.

Tingbot OS – This operating system has been designed to be used primarily with the Tingbot add-on as well as running Tide applications. This operating system is also based on the Raspbian operating system.

Tiny Core Linux – This operating system is designed to run primarily in RAM. It is a minimal Linux operating system where the primary focus is to provide a base system using BusyBox and FLTK.

Void Linux – This operating system is a rolling release Linux distribution that has been designed and implemented from scratch. Void Linux provides images based on musl or glibc.

WTware for Raspberry Pi – This is a free operating system that is used for the creation of Windows thin client.

Xbian – This operating system uses the Kodi open source digital media center.

Not Linux Based Operating Systems:

Genode OS Framework – This operating system is a toolkit that is used to build highly secure special purpose operating systems. This is not the operating system that would be best for those who are just starting out, however, if you have a lot of experience with coding, this is a good choice.

HelenOS – This operating system is a portable multi-server that is microkernel-based.

NetBSD – This operating system is another that will allow you to create the coding and use your Raspberry Pi 3 – Model B however, you decide.

Plan 9 – This is an open source operating system that is similar to Unix. It was originally developed at Bell Labs as a research operating system. When you are using Plan 9, everything is treated as a file regardless of whether it is a local or network resource.

Xv6 – This is a modern version of the Sixth Edition Unix operating system that has been re-implemented for teaching purposes. It is easily ported to the Raspberry Pi from MIT xv6 which can be booted from NOOBS (New Out of Box Software).

Media Center Operating Systems – If you are looking for operating systems that are going to run your Raspberry Pi 3 – Model B as a media center

18

your best options are OSMC, OpenELEC, LibreELEC, XBIAN, and Rasplex.

Audio Operating Systems – If you want to use your Raspberry Pi 3 – Model B for audio, the best operating systems are going to include Volumio, Pimusicbox, Runeaudio, and moOdeaudio.

Retrogaming Operating Systems – If you want to use your Raspberry Pi 3 – Model B to play retro games, the ideal operating systems include Retropie, Recalbox, Happi Game Centre, Lakka, ChameleonPi, and Piplay.

Driver APIs

Raspberry Pi 3 – Model B has the capability to use a VideoCore IV GPU through a binary blob. The binary blob is loaded into the GPU when it is booted from the SD card. Much of the driver work was originally done using the closed source GPU code, although there are software applications such as OpenMAX, OpenGL ES, or OpenVG which can be used to call an open course driver in the VideoCore IV GPU driver code.

Firmware

The official firmware of the Raspberry Pi 3 – Model B is a closed course binary blob that is freely redistributable. There is also open source firmware that is available minimally.

Third Party Application Software

As well as the operating systems that we covered in this chapter, there are many options for other software that can be put onto your Raspberry Pi 3 – Model B from third parties. In this section, we are going to briefly look at some of the more popular third party applications.

Mathematica – Raspbian includes a full installation of this software for free. This allows programs to be run from either a command line interface or from a notebook interface. Some of the language functions allow for accessing connected devices.

Minecraft – In February 2013, a version of Minecraft was released for Raspberry Pi that allows you to modify the game world with code. This is the only official version of Minecraft that allows this.

RealVNC – RealVNC's remote access server and viewer software are included with the Raspbian operating system. This includes the new capture technology which allows content to be directly rendered as well as non-X11 applications to be viewed and controlled remotely.

UserGate Web Filter – In 2013, Entensys, a security vendor based in Florida, announced they would be porting Usergate Web Filter to the Raspberry Pi Platform.

Software Development

In addition to the addition applications listed above, there are programs available that can help you learn more about developing software. Learning how to develop software will help you be able to use the Raspberry Pi 3 – Model B to its fullest potential.

AlgoID – This is a program that is ideal for teaching programming to children as well as beginners in the programming world.

Julia – This is a programming language that is both interactive and able to be used across multiple platforms. IDE's for Julia are also available including June and JuliaBerry, which is a Pi specific repository.

Scratch – This teaching tool uses visual blocks that stack to teach IDE. MIT's Life Long Kindergarten group originally developed this. The version that was created for Pi is heavily optimized for the limited computing resources that are available and work well with the Squeak Smalltalk system.

Now that you are aware of the software options that are available for you to use with your Raspberry Pi 3 – Model B, we are going to explore how you can go about configuring your Raspberry Pi to do what you want it to do.

Chapter 4: Configuring Raspberry Pi

Once you have your Raspberry Pi 3 – Model B in your possession, you are going to want to get it set up and ready to use. The good news is that setting it up is easy and takes less than thirty minutes. That means that before you know it, you are going to be ready to start doing some awesome stuff with your new piece of technology!

Before You Start

Before you get started, there are a few supplies you are going to need on hand in addition to the Raspberry Pi to get through the set-up process and move on to amazing projects.

HDMI television or monitor – You are going to need to connect your Raspberry Pi to a display which means that you need some sort of HDMI enabled screen. You don't need to use a full-sized monitor for your Raspberry Pi, and there are compact options on the market. There are also ways around using a monitor at all, which we will discuss later in this chapter.

USB keyboard and mouse – In order to be able to control your Raspberry Pi 3 – Model B, you are going to need to have a keyboard and mouse. Any USB keyboard and mouse will work for this.

8GB MicroSD card and card reader – Instead of using a hard drive, Raspberry Pi's operating system is installed with a MicroSD card. You are going to want at least 8Gb for this. Your computer might have a card reader. If it does not, all you are going to need is a cheap one,. Card readers can often be found for under $10 USD.

Power Supply – The Raspberry Pi 3 – Model B is powered by a micro USB, similar to the one you likely use for your cell phone. Since the Pi 3 – Model B has four USB ports, the best power supply is one that can provide at least 2.5A of power.

Step One – Install Raspbian Onto Your MicroSD Card with NOOBs

The first thing you are going to have to do before you can use your new Raspberry Pi 3 – Model B is to put Raspbian onto your MicroSD card. To do this, you first need to download the operating system on another computer and transfer it to your

SD card. There are two ways you can do this. First, you can install Raspian manually. This required you to either know the command line, or external software. The second option, which is much simpler requires that you download and install NOOBs Since this is the easier option, this is the option we are going to review in this chapter.

1 – Put your SD card into your computer or SD card reader.

2 – Download NOOBs. Choose the option of "offline and network install." This option will include Raspbian in the download itself.

3 – You may need to format your SD card as FAT. If so, download the SD Association's Formatting Tool which can be found at sdcard.org. Simply set the "Format Size Adjustment" to "on" in the options menu, and your SD card will be formatted.

4 – Extract the Zip file. Once the extraction is complete, copy the entire folder contents to your SD card. Once the copy is complete, you can eject your SD card and insert it into your Raspberry Pi 3 – Model B.

Step Two – Hook Up Your Raspberry Pi

The next step is to connect your devices to your Raspberry Pi 3 – Model B. Doing this is very easy, since all you need to do is plug stuff into the USB ports. However, it is important to do this is in the order listed below to ensure that all of your devices are recognized when you boot your Raspberry Pi up.

1 – Connect your monitor to your Raspberry Pi

2 – Connect your USB mouse and keyboard

3 – If you are using an Ethernet cable for your router, connect it now.

4 – Connect your power adapter. Since your Raspberry Pi 3 – Model B doesn't have a power switch, as soon as you connect the power source it is going to turn on.

Step Three – Set Up Raspbian

When you first boot up NOOBs, it is going to be busy for a couple of minutes formatting the SD card and setting things up. Let it do what it needs to do. Eventually, there will be a screen that will come up asking you to install an operating system.

1 – At the bottom of the screen there is going to be a place where you can select your language and keyboard layout for your region.

2 – Check the box that is next to the Raspbian option and click install.

NOOBs will then run the installation process, which can take anywhere from ten to twenty minutes.

Once it is complete, the Raspberry Pi will restart itself and then send you straight to the Raspbian desktop where you will have the ability to configure everything else.

Step Four – Configure Your Raspberry Pi 3 – Model B

Your Raspberry Pi is now mostly ready to go. In Raspbian you are going to see a start menu. In this start menu, you are going to be able to select applications, open a file browser, and execute other commands that you might expect to be able to do with an operating system. The first thing you should do is set up your Wi-Fi, as well as any Bluetooth devices you want to use, with your Raspberry Pi.

Connect to Your Wi-Fi Network

Connecting to Wi-Fi through your Raspbian is just as easy as any modern operating system you may be accustomed to working with.

1 – Click the network icon. It is located at the top right corner and looks like two computers.

2 – Select your Wi-Fi network name and enter your password.

That's it. You are now connected to your Wi-Fi network. You are only going to need to do this once, and it will work in both the command line and the graphical interface.

Connect Bluetooth Devices

If you want to use a Bluetooth enabled mouse or keyboard with your Raspberry Pi 3 – Model B, you are going to need to pair them. Depending on the device you are pairing, this process can vary a bit, but using the directions below, you shouldn't have any issues.

1 – Click on the Bluetooth icon that is in the upper right corner of your screen.

2 – Click the "Add Device" option

3 – Find the device that you want to pair your Raspberry Pi with and follow the directions that appear on the screen to pair them up.

Once you have followed the directions above, your Raspberry Pi 3 – Model B is ready for you to start playing around with. If something goes wrong and you end up somehow messing up the programming, you can also follow the above steps to reinstall Raspbian and start over.

Connect to Your Raspberry Pi Remotely

Occasionally you might find yourself in a position where you may want to access your Raspberry Pi remotely. Maybe you don't have access to a monitor, or you only have a laptop in the house. Whatever reason you may have for wanting to connect remotely, it's handy to know that there are options.

Connect to The Command Line Through SSH – You can use SSH from any computer to connect to the command line interface of your Raspberry Pi. While this option won't allow you to access a graphic interface, you can run any type of command from the Terminal application, and it'll execute on the Raspberry Pi. This is especially useful if you are working on a project that doesn't require a screen.

Use VNC To Use Your Home Computer as A Remote Screen – If your project requires that you do have a graphical interface, VNC (virtual network computing) to obtain it. You will be able to see the Raspberry Pi's desktop in a window on your computer desktop, and you will be able to control it like you are using the Pi. This isn't the best option for the day to day use as it is slow, but in the event that you only need to get a few things established and don't want to necessarily have to use the keyboard and mouse, this is an easy way to do so.

Now that you know how to get your Raspberry Pi 3 – Model B up and running, in the next chapter, we are going to look at some of the programming associated with your Raspberry Pi.

Chapter 5: Programming In Raspberry Pi

The original purpose of the Raspberry Pi was to be able to teach people about technology. In this chapter, we are going to learn some of the basics of the two programming languages that are included in Raspbian, which is the recommended distribution for the Pi.

Scratch

This is a great language for those who are learning the basics of programming. Scratch doesn't require you to get the text perfect. Instead, everything is done by dragging and dropping program blocks into your script. This also means that you aren't going to have to remember any of the commands. For this example, we are going create a simple drawing program that will allow us to use the arrow keys to trace lines on the screen.

The first thing you are going to have to do is open Scratch. You will find Scratch in the **Menu**, under

Programming. Once you have opened Scratch, you will see a screen with blocks of code, a scripts area, a stage where you can see your project, as well as some toolbars.

Now that we have the program open, we are going to create the code that will let us move the cat sprite around the screen.

We are going to use three separate blocks, each of which will be executed when a key is pressed. First, press the yellow control button, which is located on the left side of the screen near the top. Drag and drop the option "**When Space Key Pressed**" into the scripts box. This is going to create a script that will run whenever the space key is pressed. Use the drop-down menu and change **Space** to **Right Arrow**. Click on the blue motion button that is located next to the yellow control button and drag **Move 8 Steps** under **Right Arrow** in the scripts window. This will allow you to move the cat forward by pressing the right arrow.

Now that you have done that, create similar scripts that turn clockwise when the down key is pressed, and counter clockwise when the up key is pressed. Once you have finished that, we will be able to move around. However, we will need to add a block that will allow us to draw. Since we don't want to draw all the time, we will use Scratch's **pen up** and **pen down** actions. When the pen is down, the cat will leave a line behind it. When the pen is up, the catwon't.

In order to toggle between having the pen up and the pen down, we are going to require the code to remember which state the pen is in. Programs use variables to do this. A variable is a chunk of memory that allows you to place data in and read data from. Before you are going to be able to use a variable, you are going to have to tell the computer to assign memory to it. We are also going to assign it a name that we can use to refer to it in the commands.

Go to **Variables**, in the same area you found control and motion, click on **Make a Variable**, and give it the name **Pen**. Once you have done this, you are going to see a selection of commands that are able to alter or use the variable. Now that we have a way to store the date, we are going to tell the computer to change its behavior based on what the variable is. This is done using an **If... Else** block. This is going to ask if a statement is true. If it is, it will execute the first block of code. If not, it will execute the second.

In our program, we are going to take the variable, **Pen**. If it is 0, we are going to put the pen down, then set it to one. Otherwise, we will lift the pen and set it to be 0. In this way, we are going to be able to toggle between the two states by using the spacebar.

Now you can move the cat around and draw a picture. However, wouldn't it be even better if you could insert a predefined item? We are going to learn how to add circles next. Technically it is going to be a twenty-four-sided shape, but it will look similar to a circle.

The method to do this is to **move forward 10**, then **rotate 15 degrees**, then **move forward 10**, then **rotate 15 degrees**, and keep doing this until you have completed the circle, which would require you to put in the same two lines twenty-four times. This would work, but it isn't the best way. Not only would it look terrible in the coding and be time consuming, but if you wanted to change the size of the circle, you would need to do this twenty-four times. The good news is, there is a better option.

Instead of writing out the code twenty-four times, can instead use a loop. A loop is a block that repeats itself. There are different types of loops, some that will keep going until a statement becomes false, and some that execute a set number of times. For this, we are going to use one that executes a set number of times.

You can find the loop option in the yellow control tab. We are going to use just two commands: **move forward 10**, and **rotate 15 degrees.** We will then set this to happen twenty-four times.

Now that you know how to use Scratch, you can play around with Scratch and discover just how much you can do with this programming software. (Peers, 2015)

Python

While Scratch is great to help you to learn the basics of programming, sooner or later you are going to reach its limitations and want to move onto something new. Python is a popular general-purpose programming language that is also easy to learn.

The first thing you need to be aware of is that Python is entirely text-based. This doesn't mean that it is unable to create graphics, but rather that your program code is going to written text instead of the drag and drop blocks we used in Scratch.

Before you get started with Python, it is important to know that since Python is text-based, you can use any text editor to create your programs. Leafpad comes with Pi and is a great starting point. Avoid using word processors such as LibreOffice Writer as they mess up the formatting and won't allow your program to function correctly.

First, open the Pi **menu** and choose **Programming** and then **Python 3**. This is the command line, but since we want to access IDLE's text editor, we are going to choose **File** and **New** to create a new blank document. On the first line type:

#!/usr/bin/python

This line is going to tell the system to use the program python, in the folder /usr/bin/ to run the file. This is important to add to the start of all the programs you create with Python.

In the programming world, there is a long-standing tradition of having your first program output "Hello World!" and we aren't going to break it here! Leave the second line blank and on the third line type:

Print "Hello World!"

Save your work in a file called hello.py.

Skipping a line in your coding is not strictly necessary. However, it makes your code easier to read.

To run the program we just created, open a terminal and navigate to where you saved the file. The default will be your home folder. First, type the following command to tell the system the file is executable:

$ chmod a+x hello.py

Next, type this command to run your program:

$ ./hello.py

You should see Hello World! appear on the screen. This shows us that the system is running properly. However, this program is not a very useful program. (Peers, 2015)

Like we did with Scratch, we are going to add some user input. With the Python program, we are going to need to add a variable to store what the user types are. Delete the line with Hello World, leaving the top line, and add the line:

Name = raw_input('what is your name')

This line is going to create the variable name, display the prompt, "what is your name?", and store what the user types are. We must place this in inverted commas so the computer can recognize it as a single chunk of text. We are then going to be able to use this variable to make our print statement a little more personal with the line:

print 'Hello', name

Since the computer is going to run the commands in order, this one needs to be below the previous one. If you were to reverse the order they are in, the computer will register an error because we are trying to use a variable before we have even created it. You can now save the file and enter **./hello.py** at the command line to run the program.

This makes the program more functional, but leaves it relatively lifeless. In order to make it more useful, we need to add a step where the computer must look at what was inputted and perform a different task based on that input. If you recall the **If** block in Scratch, we are going to do something similar here except, we are actually going to write the code. The basic structure is going to be:

if :

code block

This must be replaced with something that can be true or false. In our case, we are going to check if the name entered is a particular value:

If name == 'Jane' :

Why ==? Computers don't deal well with ambiguity. Every symbol or word that we use can only have one meaning. Otherwise, things start to get confusing. The equal sign, "=", is used to assign a value to a variable, so we need to use something else to check the equality. Again, we are going to enclose **Jane** in inverted commas so the computer can recognize it's text. The colon tells the computer that we have finished our expression, and we are about to tell it what to do.

We may want this **If** command to run through more than one line of code. This means that we need a way to group code into blocks. This is done using indents in Python. Indents can be either a space or a tab. However, it is crucial to use the same method throughout your project to avoid confusion. Python doesn't read the amount of indentation, but rather the number of indents you have made. Personally, I use two spaces for each indent, because that's how I was taught, and it makes it simple to keep it all the same.

Back to our programming. Now we want the computer to do something **if name == 'Jane'** so we have to tell the computer what we want it to do.

if name == 'Jane' :

  print "Jane, you're awesome"

Note that there are two spaces at the start of the second line. There are also double speech marks. This is because the text we have enclosed has an apostrophe in it. Since we don't want to be rude to all the people who aren't Jane, we are going to add an else block that runs whenever the above expression is false:

else :

  print 'hello', name

One last feature we are going to include is a loop. This is going to work similar to the one we created in Scratch, except it isn't going to only run twenty-four times. Instead, it will run until we tell it to stop. We are going to do this using a while look and the syntax:

while :

code block

We can have the program stop by entering the **name quit**. This means our **while** loop will be:

while name !: 'quit' :

For some reason, exclamation marks are often used to mean "not in the programming world". However, we are still left with a bit of a problem. If we put it before **name = raw_input...** we are going to produce an error because the computer doesn't know what **name** is. But if we put it after, it will only ask us to enter a name once, then spit the greeting out indefinitely, which is also not ideal.

There is a way to solve this. We are simply going to string the name before **while**. This stops the error and will always trigger the **while** expression. So, the program should look like this:

```
#!/usr/bin/python

name = "

while name != 'quit' :
name = raw_input('What is your name?')

if name == 'Jane' :
    print "Jane, you're awesome"
else :
    print 'Hello', name
```

You should note that there are four spaces before each print line. This is because they have been indented twice. Once for the **while** loop and once for the **if** statement. Now you can save this as hello.py and as before, run it with ./hello.py.

Both Scratch and Python are great programs to get started with, so now you can pick the one that appealed to you the most. In the next chapter, we are going to look at some sample project ideas that you can use to get started with programming your Raspberry Pi 3 – Model B.

Chapter 6: Sample Project Ideas For Your Raspberry Pi

Now you know all the technical information about your Raspberry Pi 3 – Model B, as well as some of the basics about using it for programming. From here we are going to go over some sample projects you can do, or build off of, as you begin to learn all that your Raspberry Pi can do.

Turn Your Raspberry Pi into A Wireless Access Point

There are many different reasons you might want to turn your Raspberry Pi into a wireless access point. Here are some of the most common reasons:

- Extend your existing Wi-Fi Network;
- Learn more about wireless networking;
- Create a free Access Point;
- Build a honey trap to learn about network hardening;
- Learn about sniffing packets;
- Provide guest wireless access that is firewalled through your main network;

- Closed Wi-Fi monitoring station for weather recording, temperature sensing; and
- Create a Raspberry Pi Hot Spot.

The first thing you need to do is ensure that your Raspberry Pi 3 – Model B is all set up and ready to be used. Assuming that it is, you are now going to run **sudo raspi-config** and set up your Pi, changing your memory split to sixteen. You are then going to reboot and set a password, if you choose to, for the root user.

Assuming that you are logged in under Root User, you are now going to install Aptitude with **apt-get install aptitude**. Once this is installed, you are going to use the command **aptitude update; aptitude safe-upgrade**. The speed of your internet is what will determine how long this process is going to take.

Once that has finished, you are going to install a few packages:

Aptitude install rfkill zd1211-firmware hostapd-utils iw dnsmasq

These are:

rfkill – Wireless utility

zd1211-firmware – Software for dealing with zd1211 based wireless hardware

44

hostapd – This is the hostap wireless access point

hostap-utils – These are the tools that go with hostap

iw – Wireless configuration utility

dnsmasq – A DHCP and DNS utility

An addition option is to add **vim** to that list. Vim is a nicer console editor than the default vi.

Next, you are going to locate the file /etc/dhcpcd.conf. Once you have found this file, you are going to add these lines to the end:

interface wlano

static ip_address=192.168.1.1/24

static routers=192.168.0.1

static domain_name_servers=8.8.8.8

8.8.4.4

These lines are going to instruct dhcpcd to statically configure the WLANO interface with an IP address. You can change this IP address to whatever you are intending to use for your wireless network.

However, you must leave the /24 as it is important and the coding will not work without it. At this time, you should change the gateway from the default 192.168.0.1 to whatever the gateway is on your normal LAN which the wired ETHO interface is connected to. Leave the domain_name_servers as is, that's the Google DNS farm and should always work.

The next thing we are going to do is configure hostap. We are going to edit /etc/hostapd/hostapd.conf to look like this:

interface=wlan0
driver=nl80211
ssid=test
channel=1

Ensure that you don't leave any spaces at the end of each line, as hostap is very literal in reading its configuration and spaces will alter how the language is being read.

Finally, you are going to configure dnsmasq to allow yourself to obtain an IP address from your new Pi Point. Edit /etc/dnsmasq.conf to look like this:

 # Never forward plain names (without a dot or domain part)
domain-needed

 # Only listen for DHCP on wlan0
interface=wlan0

 # create a domain if you want, comment it out otherwise
#domain=Pi-Point.co.uk

Create a dhcp range on your /24 wlan0 network with 12 hour lease time
dhcp-range=192.168.1.5,192.168.1.254,255.255.255.0,12h

Send an empty WPAD option. This may be REQUIRED to get windows 7 to behave.
#dhcp-option=252,"\n"

Remember that you are going to change the dhcp-range to match the network IP address you are using. To ensure that your Pi Point is going to work after it is rebooted, you are going to need to create a run file that will turn on forwarding, nat and run hostap at the time of booting. To do this you are going to create a file named /etc/init.d/pipoint with the following contents:

```sh
#!/bin/sh
# Configure Wifi Access Point.
#
### BEGIN INIT INFO
# Provides: WifiAP
# Required-Start: $remote_fs $syslog $time
# Required-Stop: $remote_fs $syslog $time
# Should-Start: $network $named slapd
```

autofs ypbind nscd nslcd

Should-Stop: $network $named slapd

autofs ypbind nscd nslcd

Default-Start: 2

Default-Stop:

Short-Description: Wifi Access Point

configuration

Description: Sets forwarding, starts

hostap, enables NAT in iptables

END INIT INFO

turn on forwarding

echo 1 > /proc/sys/net/ipv4/ip_forward

enable NAT

iptables -t nat -A POSTROUTING -j

MASQUERADE

start the access point

hostapd -B /etc/hostapd/hostapd.conf

Next make the script executable with **chmod +x /etc/init.d/pipoint** and add the script to the startup sequence of the Raspberry Pi using **update-rc.d pipoint start 99 2**. This will ensure that your Pi Point will reboot itself as a functioning Wi-Fi access point.

Turn Your Raspberry Pi 3 – Model B Into A Retro Arcade Machine

Who doesn't love retro video games? This project is going to show you how to very simply turn your Raspberry Pi into a retro games console in no time. First, open up a terminal window. You can find this at the top of the screen. Once it's open, type **sudo apt-get update** followed by **sudo apt-get install -y git dialog**. Next, you are going to type **cd** and then **git clone git://github.com/petrockblog/RetroPie-Setup.git**. This is going to download a little script that is going to install tons of game emulators for you. To prepare the installer, type: **cd RetroPie-Setup**, then **chmod +x retropie_setup.sh**.

In the same terminal window, we are going to type: **sudo./retropie_setup.sh**, this is going to run the installer and bring up an awesome retro interface. Once we are here, we are going to select the binaries-based install option. This is going to take about an hour.

Once this is installed, we are going to open up another terminal window and type: **sudo raspi-config**. In this configuration app, you are going to go into the boot options and choose to make the Pi boot into a command prompt instead of Raspbian. Now you are going to reset the Pi, and then type

EmulationStation to run your new retro game center.

This is going to give you access to emulators for more than twenty systems, including the Mega Drive and Nintendo 64. While some games are going to be built in, you are going to have to check out a site like *emuparadise*.

Create A Media Center With Your Raspberry Pi

Before you get started on making your Raspberry Pi into a media center, you are going to need to obtain a few components:

- Raspberry Pi Case
- Standard SD card
- Micro-USB cable and wall charger
- HDMI cable
- USB mouse and keyboard

The first thing you are going to do is get your Raspberry Pi set up in the case. The board should fit snugly in the case without needing to be forced in. Once you have placed your Raspberry Pi into your case and screwed the top on, you are ready to move on.

The media center is going to run on RaspBMC Linux distribution, and you are going to need to download this from a computer other than the Raspberry Pi. Once you unzip the file, right click the file **setup.exe** and select "Run as Administrator" click yes to the User Account Control dialog. You will then be presented with an interface which will allow you to install the RaspBMC to an SD card. Next, select the SD card from the list and check the box stating that you agree with the license agreement and select install.

Now that the software has been installed on the SD card, you are going to insert it into the Raspberry Pi. Turn the Raspberry Pi on and begin the installation process. This can take up to forty-five minutes.

Now that RaspBMC has been installed, you are going to be given the option to choose a language, and will then be greeted with the home screen. Scroll over to the program section and select the RaspBMC settings option. This is going to allow you to change your connection type from wired to wireless. You are going to be able to change many other settings to personalize your experience.

Now you are ready to add your media. Since it is impractical to store your media on the SD card, we are going to be streaming the media from an existing computer.

Go to the home menu and navigate to the video option. Here, you should see a drop-down option for files, choose this option and then click the option to add videos. This should give you a menu that allows you to browse for a source.

Select browse. A screen will appear that contains a variety of options to connect. XBMC facilitates a number of different connection options. However, most computers are going to rely on the Windows Samba option, which you will find near the bottom. Once you have clicked on this option, it is going to ask you for the username and password for the computer you are trying to stream from. Enter this information, and you will be able to view the files that you have chosen to share. Now that you have added your media, you should be able to select the media and begin streaming content.

There are three different methods you can use to control the device you have just created.

1 – A wireless mouse is one option, although it is also the most inconvenient.

2 – There are various apps you can get for your Android or iPhone.

3 – A universal remote. This is the most ideal option since you likely already have one of these in your home.

There are many, many more things you can do with your new Raspberry Pi 3 – Model B. We've walked through two of the most popular, and easiest, things you can do. Below is a list of other things that your Raspberry Pi is capable of. Feel free to attempt any of these projects, or create one of your very own, the only limit with the Raspberry Pi is your imagination.

Other Raspberry Pi Projects
- Write your own game
- Make a Gameboy (advanced)
- Make a Kodi streamer
- Build a download hub
- Create a dedicated Minecraft machine
- Build a camera trap
- Build a case for your Raspberry Pi
- Control your stereo wirelessly
- Create your own cloud server
- Make a phone
- Make a PiRate radio station
- Build a smart beer fridge
- Make a PiCam
- Make a talking toy
- Make a bitcoin mining machine

- Create a tiny arcade
- Build your own virtual assistant, similar to Amazon's Alexa
- Build a Raspberry Pi laptop
- Stream PC games to the Pi
- Raspberry Pi music player
- Raspberry Pi photo frame
- Make a motion sensor
- Raspberry Pi security camera network
- Build a Samba server
- Create a smart mirror

As you can see, the options of what you can do with the Raspberry Pi are virtually endless. Choose a project to get started with, and remember, if something ever goes wrong, simply go back to the beginning and reprogram your Raspberry Pi as if it were brand new.

Chapter 7: Accessories For Your Raspberry Pi 3 – Model B

Costing only $35, the Raspberry Pi is a great price, and it also very basic. However, there are many accessories you can get for your Raspberry Pi if you want to spend the money. In this chapter, we are going to briefly look at some of the available accessories and the pros and cons of each one. We are also going to take a look at what you would get from each accessory, whether that be aesthetic, functionality or something else.

Raspberry Pi 3 Starter/Media Center Kit – For anyone who is buying the Pi 3, particularly if it is the first Pi owned, a starter kit can be a huge benefit. It comes with a power supply, a case, an 8GB micro SD card, HDMI and Ethernet cables. It also includes NOOBs, Raspbian, and Kodi pre-installed.

HDMI to VGA Adapter – HDMI is very common. However, it's still not everywhere. If you have a monitor that is not HDMI enabled, or you just prefer VGA, this is one attachment that will make your life a lot easier.

Raspberry Pi Heatsink – The Raspberry Pi 3 – Model B produces heat. If you are going to be doing advanced projects, it is going to produce more heat. To extend the life of the processor, a heatsink is a great option.

Raspberry Pi Touchscreen – Touchscreens are everywhere, and if you are planning on making a Pi Phone or tablet, this is a great product to have. While most of the touchscreens you are going to find are only 480p, it is still better than a non-touch display.

Camera Module – Almost every device available these days has a camera. Adding a camera to your Raspberry Pi will allow you to use it as a video calling box, home security system or even as an actual camera.

Pi Sense Hat – There are some things you probably never considered you might need. Like temperature sensors, humidity sensors and an LED sensor. The PiSense Hat also has an accelerometer, a magnetic sensor, a five-button joystick, and a barometer. This makes it an essential tool for many projects.

Adafruit RGB Matrix – If you are hoping to make a stunning light show, or just need a basic display to showcase things, this fully programmable color LED board is your ideal gadget.

Adafruit Perma Promo Hat – This is a basic tool that will allow you to create and test your own custom circuits for use in your projects.

PaPiRus eink Display Hat – This is perfect if you are looking for a basic display that isn't going to suck up a bunch of power. This display is great to display a calendar, clock, or thermometer.

<u>Mini Wireless Keyboard And Mouse Touchpad</u> – This is great if you don't want to keep your Pi connected to a mouse and keyboard all the time. You aren't going to want to use this when you are typing out long strands of commands. However, it is great if you are only typing a few sudo commands or small mouse movements.

<u>Cases</u> – There are many different cases you can get for your Raspberry Pi. From the simplest cases that are used just to protect your Raspberry Pi from the elements, to cases that include a touchscreen holder or even mount to a monitor.

As you can see, there are many different options for accessories for your Raspberry Pi. Most of the accessories you are going to find listed above are available for under one hundred dollars. This means that even if you choose to invest in a few of your favorites, you are still going to be spending less than you would be on a traditional computer, and you are going to be able to do so much more with it.

Conclusion

Now that you know the basics of the Raspberry Pi 3 – Model B, you are ready to venture out and start getting some hands-on experience with it. Remember, there is a ton of different software options that you can use when you are programming your Raspberry Pi, so you are by no means confined to the ones that came standard with the Raspbian that we downloaded in the walkthroughs.

Remember, the Raspberry Pi computers were created to give everyone an affordable option to learn about technology and how they can manipulate it. Use your imagination and enjoy the process of learning how to program your Raspberry Pi 3 – Model B to do virtually anything you want it to do.

I would like to thank you for downloading my book: *Raspberry Pi: The Blueprint for Raspberry Pi 3: Everything You Need to Know For Starting Your Own Projects*. I hope you found the content in this book to be a valuable contribution to what you are going to do with your Raspberry Pi.

Bibliography

Peers, B. E. (2015, December 29). Retrieved March 1, 2017, from http://www.techradar.com/news/software/learn-to-program-your-raspberry-pi-1148194

The Blueprint to Python Programming

A Beginners Guide: Everything You Need to Know to Get Started

By: CyberPunk Architects

Introduction

There are many people who are interested in getting into the world of coding. They want to learn some of the basics so that they can work on their own programs, learn how to work more on their own computers, or even get started on doing work for other people. But there are many different coding languages that you can learn to work with and sometimes this can be confusing to learn which is right for you. This guidebook is going to spend some time talking about the Python coding language, one of the best languages to learn as a beginner for its ease of use as well as all its power.

In this guidebook, you are going to learn about the Python coding language. We will start with some of the basics, including learning how to install the software, as well as the right IDE and text editor so that you are able to write some of your own code. We will then move on to some of the basics of this language that you would like to include inside your codes to make them work the best. And then we move on to handling the exceptions in Python, working with loops to get a block of code to repeat without having to rewrite it a bunch of times, and the conditional statements that will make decisions for you regardless of the answer that your user places into the code.

The Python language is one of the easiest coding languages to learn how to use. It is designed for the beginner with all of the power that you are looking for inside a new coding language. This guidebook is going to take some time to help you as a beginner learn more about coding with this language so you can create some of your own codes and really join the coding community.

Chapter 1: Getting to Know the Python Program

Getting started with a new programming language can be a bit scary. You want to make sure that you are picking out one that is easy to use so that you can understand what is going on inside of the program. But you may also have some big dreams of what you want to accomplish with the programming and want an option that is able to keep up with that. The good news is that the Python programming language is able to help with all of this and is the perfect coding language for a beginner to get started with.

There are many reasons why you would enjoy working with the Python language. It is easy to learn, is meant for beginners, and it works with some of the other coding languages that you may want to learn to add in more power. It is based on the English language so there are not going to be too many issues with learning difficult words, and it has a lot of the power that you need without all the complicated make-up of other coding languages. As you will see in a minute, the syntax in Python is really easy to learn and there are a lot of powerful things that you can do with this coding language, even as a beginner.

The Python library is going to be a great help to you as you get started with this language. It has many of the syntaxes and examples that you need to help you out when you get stuck or when you have some issues figuring out how to complete some steps in Python. The community with this coding language is large as well, due to the fact that this is an easy code to work with and is great for beginners, so you will be able to find others to ask questions of or you can read through forums to learn more about the projects you want to work on.

If you are interested in getting started with the Python language, there are a few things that you will need to have on hand to make the process easier. First, you will need to make sure that the right text editor is in place on your computer. This is important because it is the software that you need to use in order to write out the codes to use inside of Python. The text editor doesn't have to be high end or complicated, and in fact, using the free Notepad option on any Windows computer, or another of this nature, will work just fine.

Once you have chosen the text editor that you would like to use, you will be able to download the actual Python program to use. The nice thing about this is that Python is free to download, as is the IDE and the other options that you will need, so you won't have to worry about the financial aspect of it. To get the Python program set up, you will just need to visit the Python website and choose the version that you would like to use.

While you are getting the Python program set up on your computer, you will also need to make sure that you download the IDE in the same instance. The IDE is basically the environment that you are going to be working in, and it will include the compiler that you need to interpret the codes that you are writing. It is often best to use the one that comes with the Python programming because this one is designed to work the best, but if you are used to working with a different IDE, you will be able to use that one as well.

If you find that there are times that you have questions about using this coding language, such as how to work on a particular code or if you are lost about why something isn't working, you should take the time to visit a Python community. The Python language has been around for some time, and it is one of the most popular coding languages in use, so the communities are pretty large. You should be able to find many groups of beginners and those who are more advanced who will be able to help you with your questions or any of the concerns that you have while learning this language.

Some of the basic parts of the Python code

Now that you have some of the Python software all set up and ready to go, it is time to work on some of the basics that come with this code. There are a lot of different parts that work together to write some amazing codes inside of Python, but learning about these basics will make it a bit easier to handle and when getting into some of the more complex processes later on. Here are some of the basics that we are going to concentrate on first before moving to some of the harder stuff later on:

Keywords

Any coding software that you use is going to have some keywords. These are words that will tell the interpreter what you want to happen in the code, so they are important to be familiar with. It is recommended that you do not use these anywhere else in your code in order to avoid confusion or error when the interpreter gets ahold of it, considering these are major action words. Some of the keywords that you should look at when working in the Python language include:

- False
- Finally
- Class
- Is
- Return
- Continue
- None
- For
- Try
- True
- Lambda
- Def
- Nonlocal
- From

- While
- Global
- Del
- And
- Not
- Raise
- In
- Except
- Break
- Pass
- Yield
- As
- If
- Elif
- Or
- Import
- Assert
- Else
- Import

This is a good list to keep on hand when you are writing your codes. This will help you to send the right information to the interpreter when you are writing through the code. Any time that you see an error message come up after writing out code make sure to check if you used one of those words properly within your statements.

Names of Identifiers

While working on a new code or program with Python, you will need to work with a few different things including variables, functions, entities, and classes. These will all have names that are also called identifiers. When you are creating the name of an identifier, regardless of the type you are working on, some of the rules that you should follow include:

- You should have letters, both lower case and upper casework are acceptable, the underscore symbol, and numbers. You are able to choose any combination of these as well. Just make sure that there are no spaces between characters.
- You can never start an identifier with a number. You are able to use something

like "sixdogs," but "6dogs" would not be acceptable.

- The identifier should not be one of the keywords that were listed above, and there should never be one of the keywords inside of it.

If you do go against one of these rules, you will notice that a syntax error will occur and the program will close on you. In addition to the rules above, you should ensure that the identifiers are easy to read for the human eye. This is important because while the identifier may follow the rules that were set out above, they can still have trouble when the human eye isn't able to understand what you are writing out.

When you are creating your identifier, make sure that you pick one that will be descriptive. Going with one that will describe what the code is doing or what the variable contains is a good place to start. You should also be wary of using abbreviations because these aren't always universally understood and can cause some confusion.

Chapter 2: Some of the Basic Commands You Should Know in Python

In addition to the things that we discussed above pertaining to the Python language, there are some other things that you can put into your codes to make them really strong. There are many options and functions that you can incorporate into the codes in order to do things like: tell other programmers what to do inside the code, add similar parts with the same characteristics together, and so much more. Let's take some time to look at the different commands that you are able to use in your codes with Python and what they all mean.

Comments

Comments are a great thing to know how to use inside of Python. They allow you to leave little notes inside of the code for yourself or for other coders who want to take a look at what you are doing. The compiler is set up to not recognize these comments, this way you are able to put in as many comments as you would like without it affecting how the code is going to execute.

Python makes it really easy to add in these comments. You will simply need to use the "#" sign in front of the comment that you want to leave inside the code. Once you are done with the comment that you want to leave, you just need to hit the return button and start out on a new line so that the compiler knows that you are starting on a new part of the code. As mentioned, you are able to leave as many of these little notes inside of your code as you would like, but try to keep them just to the ones that are needed in order to keep the code looking nice and organized.

Statements

Another thing that you are able to add into your code is statements. Whenever you are working on a code, you will need to leave these statements inside of your code so that the compiler has some idea of what you would like to have shown up on the screen. A statement is going to basically be a unit of code that you can send over to the interpreter. Then your interpreter will look at the statement that you want to use and then execute it based on the command that you are giving it.

When you work on writing the code, you can choose how many statements you are able to write at one time. You can choose to just have one statement that is inside of your code, or you can have several of them based on what you would like to have happen inside of the code. As long as you keep the statements inside of the brackets inside the code and you use all the correct rules when you are writing out that part of the code, you will be able to include as many of these statements as needed into the code.

When you choose to add in a statement (or more than one statement) into the code, you will send it through to the interpreter, which is then going to work to execute the commands that you want, just as long as you make sure that you put everything else in the right place. The results of your statements will then show up on the screen when you execute it, and you can always go back in and make changes or adjustments as needed. Let's look at an example of how this would work when using statements in your code:

x = 56
Name = John Doe
z = 10

print(x)
print(Name)
print(z)

When you send this over to the interpreter, the results that should show up on the screen are:

56
John Doe

10

It is as simple as that. Open up Python and give it a try to see how easy it is to just get a few things to show up in your interpreter.

Working with variables

Variables are a good thing to learn about the inside of the Python code because they can be used to store your code in specific parts of your computer. So basically, you will find these variables are just spots on the memory of your computer that will be reserved for the values of the code that you are working on. When you are working on the variables in the code, you are telling the computer to save some room on its memory to store these variables. Depending on what type of data you would like to use in the code, the variable is able to tell the computer what space should be saved on that location.

Giving the variable a value

In order to make the variables work inside the code, you need to make sure that they get a value assigned to each. Otherwise they are just basic places on the memory. You need to put some kind of value to the variable in order to get it to work properly, so it reacts inside the code. There are two types of variables that you will be able to use, and the one that you choose will determine the value type that you give to it. The different types of variables that we can pick from include:

Float: this would include numbers like 3.14 and so on.

String: this is going to be like a statement where you could write out something like "Thank you for visiting my page!" or another similar phrase.

Whole number: this would be any of the other numbers that you would use that do not have a decimal point.

When you are using this program, you will not need to use declarations in order to reserve this space on the memory since this is something that will occur right when you add a value to the variable you are working with. If you want to make sure that this is going to happen automatically, you just need to use the (=) symbol so that the value knows which variable it is supposed to be working with:

Some examples of how this works include:

x = 12   *#this is an example of an integer assignment*
pi = 3.14   *#this is an example of a floating point assignment*
customer name = John Doe   *#this is an example of a string assignment*

Now at this point, we are looking at just writing the code, but what if you would like to have the interpreter execute the code that we are using. Luckily, this is pretty simple to work on. You just need to make sure that you write out the word "print" before the statement that you want to use. However, in the newer versions, such as Python 3, you would want to add in the parenthesis. Either way, this is pretty easy to learn how to do. Here is a good example of how you would be able to make this work inside Python:

print(x)

print(pi)

print(customer name)

Based on the information listed above, when this is printed out, your interpreter is going to execute the results:

12

3.14

John Doe

You are also able to add in more than one value to the same variable if this is what needs to happen for the code to work within your code. You just need to make sure that you are including the equal sign ("=") in between each of the parts to make it work the right way. For example, "a = b = c = 1" would be acceptable and makes it so that all of those variables would equal 1 inside of your code. This is just a simpler option to use rather than writing each of these out on their own and making them equal to 1.

These are just a few more of the basics that you will need to learn how to use when it comes to writing out your own codes in Python. These are pretty simple to learn how to do and you are going to enjoy all the power that they add into even the simplest codes you will be writing in the beginning.

Chapter 3: Working with Loops in Python

Now that we know some of the basics associated with working on the Python language, it is time to move into some of the more complex parts of this language and learn how to make it all work for your program. With the other options included in this guidebook, we talk about decision control instructions or sequential control instructions. When we are working with the decision control options (which will be discussed in the following chapter), we are putting the calculations into a fixed order to be figured out. With the sequential option, the interpreter is going to execute your instructions based on how your conditions will turn up at the end. There are a few limitations that come up with these options, mostly because they are only able to do the action once.

Now, what happens if you would like to have the action done more than once? With the other options that we discussed in this book, this would mean that you would need to rewrite the code over and over again until it is repeated as many times as you would like it to be. But what happens when you want to make something like a table that counts from 1 to 100? Do you want to write out the same part of code 100 times to make this happen?

Luckily, there are some options within Python that can be used to make it easier to write out these things as many times as you would like, while only taking up a few lines. These are called "loops," and they ensure that you are able to repeat the code as many times as you would like, from one to a thousand or higher if you would like. They are much easier to write out, they can save you a lot of time, and they will basically ensure that you are going to get the loop to continue until the conditions of the code are no longer true.

At first, you may feel that these loops are going to be kind of complicated because you have to tell the program how to repeat itself over and over as many times as you want, but it is actually pretty simple. There are three different types of loops that you can use inside of Python depending on what you would like the code to do. The three loops that you are able to use include the "while" loop, the "for" loop, and the "nesting" loop. Each of the loops is going to work in a different way to help you to repeat the part of the code that you need as many times as needed. Let's take a look at how each of these work, and when you would choose to use each one inside of your code.

What is the while loop?

The first loop that we are going to take a look at is the while loop. This is a good one to start on when you would like to make the code repeat itself, or go through the same actions, a fixed amount of times. For example, if you want to make sure that the loop goes through the same steps ten times, you would want to use the while loop. But if you would like to use this to create an indefinite number of loops, this is not the option to go with.

One of the examples that you would want to use with the while loop is when calculating out the amount of interest that is owed or paid. You can do this several times in order to find the perfect option for your user, but this one can be set up so that the user will not have to go back through the program multiple times and get frustrated. Here is a good example that you can use in order to learn how the while loop statements are going to work when you would like to calculate simple interest:

#calculation of simple interest. Ask user to input principal, rate of interest, number of years.

```
counter = 1
while(counter <= 3):
        principal   =   int(input("Enter   the
principal amount:"))
        numberofyeras = int(input("Enter   the
number of years:"))
        rateofinterest = float(input("Enter   the
rate of interest:"))
        simpleinterest    =    principal    *
numberofyears * rateofinterest/100
        print("Simple   interest   =   %.2f"
%simpleinterest)
        #increase the counter by 1
        counter = counter + 1
        print("You   have   calculated   simple
interest for 3 time!")
```

With this particular loop, the user will be able
to put in the numbers they want to use for
interest three times. After they are done, it will
be set up to have a message show up on the
screen. You can make this more complicated if
you would like, adding in more lines for the
user to input their answer as many times as

they choose. The user of the program will be the one in charge, choosing how much they want to put into each of the spots. The user will be able to redo this program as well, starting over at the beginning, if they would like to add in more than the three interest spots than what they have in right now.

Working with the for loop

Now that we understand a bit more about the while loop, it is time to move on to the for loop. This one will work similarly to the other loop, but is a more traditional way to work with loops. If you have worked in any other coding languages in the past, you may be more familiar with this particular loop. If you do plan to use Python with another coding language, you should consider using the for loop to make things easier.

When using the for loop, the user will not be the one who defines the conditions that will make the loop stop. The Python program is going to make the statement continue repeating, in the exact order that it is placed inside your statement. Below you will find an example of how the for loop would work inside your code:

```
# Measure some strings:
words = ['apple', 'mango', 'banana', 'orange']
for w in words:
print(w, len(w))
```

Take some time to insert these statements into your compiler. With this one, the four fruits that are in this code, or the other statements that you choose to use, will repeat in the order that you write them out. If you are writing out this particular code and you want to make sure that they come out in a different order than what is listed above, you will need to make sure that you turn them around when writing the code. The computer will not take the time to make the changes and it is not going to allow you to change these at all when you are working on the actual code.

On the other hand, if you are looking for the loop to just go through a certain sequence of numbers or words, such as only wanting the first three fruits to show up on the screen, you will find that using your range() function is the best one for this. This function is going to generate a big list of the arithmetic progressions that you can use inside of the code to help make this easier.

The nested loops

The third type of loop that we are going to take a look at is the nested loop. This one is going to sound a bit more complicated than you are used to with the other two options, but the code is actually going to be shorter than the others, and all the options that you are going to be able to do with the nested loop can make it a great one to learn even as a beginner. To keep things basic, the nested loop is just a loop that is inside of another loop. Both of the loops will just keep going through the repeat process until both of the programs have time to finish.

We are going to take a moment to look at an example of working on the nested loops. We are going to use the idea of a multiplication table in order to show you how several loops inside your code will be able to bring up a lot of information and you will only need to have a few lines of code to make this happen. The code that we are going to write will make the multiplication table go from 1 up to 10. Here is the example that you are able to use:

#write a multiplication table from 1 to 10
For x in xrange(1, 11):
For y in xrange(1, 11):
*Print '%d = %d' % (x, y, x*x)*

When you get the output of this program, it is going to look similar to this:

1*1 = 1
1*2 = 2
1*3 = 3
1*4 = 4
1*5 = 5

This would continue going until you got all the way up to 1*10 = 2
Then it would move on to do the table by twos such as this:

2*1 =2

```
2*2 = 4
2*3 = 6
```

For this one, you are going to keep on going until you end up with 10*10 and the answer that goes with this. You will have a complete multiplication table without having to write out the lines that go with each one, which makes this whole process easier to handle. Just look at the code above, there are only four lines (one of which is a comment), and you can get a table that is pretty complete and long. This is just one of the samples of what you are able to do and one of the main reasons that people will choose to go with loops rather than trying to write out all of the lines that they need.

Loops are one of the best things that you can work on when it comes to being inside the Python language. It can simplify the code that you are working on and ensures that you are able to get a lot of stuff done inside the code without having too much information written out and making it look like a mess. Try out a few of these loop options in your code and see what a difference they can make.

Chapter 4: Handling Exceptions in Your Code

There are times when you will need to work with exceptions when working inside the code. These can work one of two ways. For the first one, it is an exception that the program doesn't like, such as trying to divide a number by zero. When this happens, an error is going to come up on the screen, but you will be able to change the message that comes up on the screen with this to help avoid issues and to make sure that your user has some idea of what the issue is. Then there are exceptions that are particular to your program. If you do not want to allow your user to put in a certain number or another input, you would want to raise an exception to make this not allowed.

So any time that you would like to show the user that a condition is considered abnormal within the code, you will want to bring out the exceptions. There are several types of these that show up inside of the code, and some of which are as simple as writing out the code the wrong way or using the incorrect spelling that will cause the errors.

Any time that you are working in your Python program, and you want to make sure that you are bringing up the exceptions in the proper way, you will want to check out the Python library. There are several of these exceptions that are already in place inside the library and will save you a lot of time. It can be extremely beneficial when you check these exceptions out first. There are several exception types that you are able to use inside this language, including whenever you are dividing a number by zero, or whenever you try to reach a part that is outside the end of the file.

Exceptions can be a nice thing to work with within Python. The nice thing is that you aren't stuck dealing with the error messages that come up on a code. You can change them up a bit to help explain what is going on to the user so that any confusion can be bypassed. When an error message comes up on the screen, it can be difficult to determine what is wrong, especially if your user has no experience working with coding at all. But when you can make some changes, such as adding in a message like "you are trying to divide by zero!" it can explain what is going on with the error so the user can correct or change their process, and makes your code a bit more user-friendly.

You are also able to make some of your own exceptions if the code you are writing asks for it. You will not be able to find these inside of the Python library, but it is still an option that you are able to use. You will need to create some of these on your own so that an error, which can be a message like you did with the ones that were found in the library, will make things easier for the user to understand why the error is showing up.

When you are trying to write out exceptions within the Python language, there are a few things that you are going to find inside of your Python library in which you should take a bit of time to look over and learn how to work with. If you would like to work on the exceptions, you will need to make sure that you learn some of the key terms that need to be present to tell the compiler what you are doing. There are many options to choose from, but some of the statements that are best for working inside of your code with exceptions inside of Python coding include:

- Finally: with this one, you will be able to bring up the word to do the cleanup actions. This is a good one to use whether the user brings up the exception or not.
- Assert: this is the condition that is used whenever you would like to trigger that

an exception has occurred inside the code.

- Try/except: these are the keywords that you will want to use whenever you are trying out a block of code. It is going to be recovered because of the exception that was raised either by you or by the Python program for some other reason.

- Raise: when you use the raise command, you are working to trigger the exception outside the code, doing so manually.

These are some of the best words to use in order to work with your exceptions and to make sure also that you will get all of your errors and other parts to work within the code. Whether you want to raise an exception that is recognized by the code or you are trying to work with one that is just for your program, in particular, you will be able to use these to help make things work within the code.

Raising an exception

Now that we have taken some time to look at what exceptions are all about, it is now time to learn how to raise exceptions. This is a pretty easy concept for you to work on and understand. For example, whenever you are working with the code inside of Python, and there is some kind of issue that is coming up with it, or you see that the program is trying to do things that aren't allowed within the rules of Python, the compiler is going to raise an exception for the behavior in question. This is because the program is going to see the issue and will not be sure about how it should react.

In some cases, the exception that is going to be raised will be pretty simple and could be something like naming the code the wrong way or spelling something wrong. You will just need to go back through the code and make the changes. Or there could even be some issues with the user attempting an action that is not allowed by the code, such as when a user may try to divide by zero. Let's take a look at how this is going to work so that you can see the steps that are needed in order to raise an exception:

x = 10

y = 10

result = x/y #trying to divide by zero

print(result)

The output that you are going to get when you try to get the interpreter to go through this code would be:

>>>

Traceback (most recent call last):

   File "D: \Python34\tt.py", line 3, in <module>

   result = x/y

ZeroDivisionError: division by zero

>>>

For the example that we did above, the Python coding language is going to show an error because you were trying to take a number and divide it by zero. The Python language is one that won't allow you to do this action, and so the error is going to come up on the screen. As we mentioned above, when you see that this error is coming up, the user may be confused and not understand what is going on at all. When you use this to raise up an exception, you should consider changing up the message so that the user has some idea of what is going on so that he or she can make the correct and necessary changes so that the code will work the way that it should.

How to make your own exceptions

So far, we have spent most of our time looking at the steps that you will need to take in order to work with the exceptions that are already recognized by the system. But what happens when you would like to raise some of your own exceptions that work with your particular program that the system does not already recognize? A good example for this is when you want to make sure that your user is not able to place specific numbers into the system. You want to make sure that when the user places these numbers into the system, they are going to get an exception. Or if you would like the user to put in five numbers and they only put in four, you could use the idea of exceptions as well.

The trick with this type of action is that the Python program may not see that there is even an issue. The program is not going to realize that there is an issue with just putting in four numbers rather than the five unless you tell it that this is an issue. You will be the one who is able to set up the exceptions that you want to use, and you can mess around and add in any exception that you would like as long as it meets up with the other rules that are used inside of Python. Let's take a look at the example that is below so that we can understand how the exceptions work and to get some practice with using these:

```
class CustomException(Exception):
def_init_(self, value):
```

```
        self.parameter = value
def_str_(self):
        return repr(self.parameter)


try:
        raise    CustomException("This    is    a
CustomError!")
except CustomException as ex:
        print("Caught:", ex.parameter)
```

When you use this syntax, you will get the
message of "Caught: This is a CustomError!"
and any time that your user is on the program
and puts in the wrong information, the error
message is going to show up. This error is going
to be caught if you put the conditions into the
program the right way and it is important,
especially if you set up your own exceptions in
the code, that you place the conditions into the
code.

It is possible to add in any wording as you
would like into this part, so you can change it

up as much as you would like to help better explain to the user what the error message means or what they may be doing wrong.. Mess around with this a little bit and you will find that it is easier than ever to set up some of your own exceptions or deal with the exceptions that are going on inside of your code.

Working with exceptions is a great way to ensure that you are getting the most out of your code. There are times when the code will see an abnormal condition and will need to put up a message or you will be working on your own program, and you will want to make up some of these abnormal conditions to work with what you are doing. Take a look at some of the examples that are done inside of this chapter, and you will be able to work with any of the exceptions that you would like in Python.

Chapter 5: Conditional Statements in Python

When it comes to working with your code, there will be times when you will want to make sure that the code is going to function in a specific way based on the conditions that you set, as well as the answer that the user puts in. You can keep it simple and have only one answer as an output when the user inputs an answer that is considered true based on your conditions, or you can make it more complex so that different answers will come up based on whether the input from the user is true or false. You can also give the user multiple options to input, and they can choose from those. In this chapter, we are going to take some time to talk about the different conditional statements that will work inside the Python code, including the "if" statement, the "if else" statement and the "elif" statements.

The if statement

The first statement that we are going to work with inside of Python is the "if" statement. This is the most basic of the conditional statements, and it is often a good place to start when first learning code. But there will be some challenges when it comes to the user putting in an answer that does not agree with the conditions you set.

With the if statement, you must set the conditions and then the program will do the rest, waiting for the answer from the user. If the user puts in an answer that is considered true, based on the conditions that you set, the rest of the code will be executed. This is usually in the form of a statement of some sort showing up on the screen, and then the compiler moving on to the next part of the code. On the other hand, if the user puts in an answer that is not allowed or is considered false based on the conditions that you set, nothing is going to happen. The if statements are not set up for false answers, so the program will just stop at that point.

There are going to be some issues with this of course, but it is a good place to get started. This one will help you to see how the conditional statements are going to work and gets you some practice with the compiler, but we will look at some conditional statements that are able to look further into the work we are doing so that answers will show up regardless of the answers that are put in. Let's take a look at an example of working with the if statement to give you some practice.

```
age = int(input("Enter your age:"))
if (age <=18):
        print("You are not eligible for voting,
try next election!")
print("Program ends")
```

Let's take a look at this syntax a bit to see what is going on. With this one, when the user comes onto the site and says that their age is under 18, they will match as true with the conditions that you set. This means that the statement that you put in, the "You are not eligible for voting, try next election!", will come up on the screen.

On the other hand, if the user puts in that they are another age, such as 25, into this code, nothing is going to happen. The if statement is not set up in order to handle this issue and there are no statements that are going to show up if this situation occurs. The compiler will just stop working on the code because it is false. You will need to make some changes to the code to handle this.

For the most part, you are not going to be able to use this type of conditional statement. The user is not wrong if they enter an age that is above 18 in the example above and they aren't going to really care for it if they can't see any results after they enter their age. How would you feel if you put in an answer to a program and it just stopped? The if statement is not the most efficient method of taking care of your conditional statements, so there will be many times that you should avoid using this at all. That is where the if else statement is going to come in handy.

If else statement

As we talked about above, there are some issues that come up when using the if statement. If your user enters an answer that is considered true with the if statement, the correct part of the code will execute. But if your user enters an answer that is seen as false (even if it is true for them), they will end up with a blank screen. This can easily end up with some problems when working within your code.

This is when the if else statement is going to come in use. With this one, you are able to set up true and false conditions, and different parts of the code are going to be executed based on the answers that the user gives. Pertaining to the prior example, the user could receive an answer saying they are not able to vote if they say they are under 18. But if they input an answer of 30, they would get a second answer, such as information on their closest voting poll or another relevant piece of information.

The if else statement is going to allow for more freedom inside of your code. This makes it easier than ever before for you to handle whatever answer the user puts into the system, whether it is considered true or false. With this statement, the compiler will check the answer, and if it is seen as true for that particular one, it will execute that part of the code. But if not, it moves on to the second part of the code and executes that. You are able to expand on this, going down as many times as you would like if you want to have several different answers. Here is a good example of how you would be able to use the if else statement inside of Python:

```
age = int(input("Enter your age:"))
if (age <=18):
        print("You are not eligible for voting,
try next election!")
else
        print("Congratulations! You are eligible
to vote. Check out your local polling station to
find out more information!)
print("Program ends")
```

With this example above, there are basically two options that you can use in the statement. If the user puts in their age as being 18 or younger, the first statement is the one that is going to come up. So on the screen, they are going to see the message "You are not eligible for voting, try next election!" But if the user puts in that they are 19 or above in age, they will see a different message that says: "Congratulations! You are eligible to vote. Check out your local polling station to find out more information!". This is a simple example that shows how the user will be able to put in any age that they want and the answer corresponding to their specific input is going to show up on the screen.

This one is a basic version of what you are able to do with the if else statement. This one just has one true, and one false answer and that is all that is on the statement. But there are times when you would like to have some options that the user can choose from, or you want there to be more than one true answer. For example, let's say that you would like to have the user put their favorite color. You could have five of the else statements with blue, red, yellow, green, and white. If the user puts in one of those five colors, the statement that is with that color will come up. Add in a break part that will catch all the other colors that your user may want to pick from so that an answer comes up no matter what answer they pick out.

The if else statements are able to add a lot of great things that you can use with your codes. It allows it to make a decision inside of the code based on the conditions that you set and the

113

input that your user places into the code. It is nice to use the if else statements because you can better prepare for the various answers that your user will enter, no matter what they decide to answer, and you are all set to go.

The elif statements

One more conditional statement that we are going to talk about in this chapter is the elif statement. These are a bit different than the others, but they are nice to work with because they provide the user with a few choices that they can choose from. Each of your choices are going to have a statement or a part of the code that will execute based on the decision that your user decides to go with. If you are creating a game and would like to make sure that the user can pick from several options before going further on, the elif statement is the one that you should use. The syntax that you would want to use with the elif statement includes:

if expression1:

statement(s)

elif expression2:

statement(s)

elif expression3:

statement(s)

else:

statement(s)

This is the basic syntax that you will want to work with whenever you want to use the elif statements in Python. You can just add in some of the information that you want so that the user can see the choices and pick the numbers that they would like to go with it, or the statements that work with their choices. This is one that you will be able to expand out a bit as you need, and you can choose to have two or three options or twenty options based on what you would like to see happen with the elif statements.

Here, we are going to take some time to look at how the elif statement is able to work in your coding. With this option, we are going to list a few choices of pizzas that the user is able to pick from and the corresponding number that they are able to work with. You can always add in some more options as well, and we add in an else part that is able to catch all the other options or, in this option, that will allow them to get a drink instead of a pizza if they do not like the options that are presented to them. Let's take a look at how this would be written out in your Python compiler:

```
Print("Let's enjoy a Pizza! Ok, let's go inside Pizzahut!")
print("Waiter, Please select Pizza of your choice from the menu")
pizzachoice = int(input("Please enter your choice of Pizza:"))
if pizzachoice == 1:
        print('I want to enjoy a pizza napoletana')
elif pizzachoice == 2:
        print('I want to enjoy a pizza rustica')
elif pizzachoice == 3:
```

print('I want to enjoy a pizza capricciosa')

else:

print("Sorry, I do not want any of the listed pizza's, please bring a Coca Cola for me.")

This is a pretty simple example of the elif statement and how you would be able to incorporate it into your codes. You can easily change this up to work with whatever program or game that you would like to create. The syntax, as you can see above, is offering the user a few options of pizzas that they are able to choose. When they are using the code, they will be able to pick the number that they would like and that corresponds to the pizza they want to go with. For example, if they would like to get the pizza napoletana, they would type in the number one. If they pick number one, they would see the answer "I want to enjoy a pizza napoletana" come up on their screen. This works for any of the numbers that they would choose on this option. With this one, we have even set it up so that the user can choose to just have a drink without a pizza if this is what they prefer.

The if statements are one of the best options for you to work with. They allow the code to come up with its own decisions based on the conditions that you set up in the beginning. You can make it as simple as the code just choosing to show a result when the user input is the same as your conditions, or you can add in some other parts to match up with the answers that the user places inside the code or with the choices that they want to make. There are many things that you are able to work with when using the conditional statements and you can make them as complicated or as simple as you would like.

Conclusion

Thank you for downloading *The Blueprint to Python Programming: A Beginners Guide to Everything You Need to Know to Get Started.*

The next step is to download the program and start writing some of your very own code. Since Python is a popular coding language and is great for beginners, it won't take long for you to get started on your first projects. This guidebook provided a few great examples that you can try out to get familiar with the system, but with the help of the knowledge you gained inside and the Python community, you will be writing great codes in no time. From learning how to write out the basic syntax in Python to working with conditional statements, operators, and variables, you are well on your way to being an expert in no time.

Finally, if you found this book useful in anyway, a review on Amazon is always appreciated!